D1242497

THE
MIWOK

JENS HAAKONSEN

PowerKiDS press.

NEW YORK

Published in 2018 by The Rosen Publishing Group, Inc.
29 East 21st Street, New York, NY 10010

Editor: Theresa Morlock
Book Design: Michael Flynn
Interior Layout: Reann Nye

Photo Credits: Cover Thomas Hallstein/Alamy Stock Photo; p. 5 Ted Soqui/Corbis Historical/Getty Images; p. 6 cdrin/Shutterstock.com; p. 7 Galina Barskaya/Shutterstock.com; pp. 9, 13, 17 Jeffrey B. Banke/Shutterstock.com; p. 11 Kippy Spilker/Shutterstock.com; p. 15 dirkr/Shutterstock.com; pp. 19, 23 Courtesy of the Library of Congress; p. 20 Marilyn Angel Wynn/Nativestock/Getty Images; p. 21 https://commons.wikimedia.org/wiki/File:Miwok-Paiute_ceremony_in_1872_at_current_site_of_Yosemite_Lodge.jpeg; p. 25 Andrew Zarivny/Shutterstock.com; p. 27 https://commons.wikimedia.org/wiki/File:Franciscan_missionaries_in_California.jpg p. 29 https://commons.wikimedia.org/wiki/File:Bierstadt_Albert_Mariposa_Indian_Encampment_Yosemite_Valley_California.jpg.

Library of Congress Cataloging-in-Publication Data

Names: Haakonsen, Jens, author.
Title: The Miwok / Jens Haakonsen.
Description: New York : PowerKids Press, [2018] | Series: Spotlight on the
   American Indians of California | Includes index.
Identifiers: LCCN 2017020365| ISBN 9781538324691 (pbk. book) | ISBN
   9781508162865 (6 pack) | ISBN 9781538324660 (library bound book)
Subjects: LCSH: Miwok Indians--Juvenile literature. | Indians of North
   America--California--Juvenile literature.
Classification: LCC E99.M69 .H33 2018 | DDC 979.4/00974133--dc23
LC record available at https://lccn.loc.gov/2017020365

Manufactured in China

CPSIA Compliance Information: Batch #BW18PK For further information contact Rosen Publishing, New York, New York at 1-800-237-9932.

CONTENTS

CHAPTER ONE

WHO ARE THE MIWOK?

The name "Miwok" was first used by the Central Sierra Miwok to identify themselves. Scholars also apply the name to other native groups that speak the same language, although these people originally used many different names to identify themselves. The Miwok people can be divided into two large groups that span the state of California. The Coast Miwok and the Lake Miwok lived in the western part of the state. The Bay, Plains, and Sierra Miwok lived in the east.

When the Europeans arrived during the 16th century, there were more than 20,000 Miwok living in the California region. The Europeans thought the Miwok were **primitive** people. Today, we recognize that the Miwok way of life could be beautiful and practical. The Miwok people's abilities allowed them to prosper for thousands of years. The Miwok **culture** continues to change with the Miwok people's modern **descendants**.

This picture shows Phil Johnson, a Miwok man, talking about traditional Miwok culture at the Yosemite Museum in 2014.

CHAPTER TWO

LIVING OFF THE LAND

The places where the various Miwok groups lived provided the different kinds of **resources** they used to survive. The Coast, Lake, Bay, Plains, and Sierra Miwok developed different lifestyles based on what was available to them. The Coast Miwok lived in the areas that are now Marin and southern Sonoma Counties. The Lake Miwok lived along the shores of Clear Lake, and the Bay Miwok lived on the eastern part of San Francisco Bay. The Plains and Sierra Miwok lived inland and depended on land resources.

This photograph shows the California Bay Area as it appears today.

Nearly all of the Miwok's lands were filled with elk, deer, and bear. Those who lived near the coast also hunted sea otters, seals, and sea lions. The lakes, rivers, and streams offered fish and shellfish. The Miwok gathered many kinds of plants to make food and tools. They also ate acorns, mushrooms, and berries.

CHAPTER THREE

HOW THEY COOKED

The Miwok used a number of tools and methods to prepare food. Nuts were crushed and ground using stone tools, including flat slabs called metates and rocks with round holes called mortars. The ground nuts were sometimes used as flour. Cooking pits were used to roast food. These pits were made by digging a hole in the ground and building a fire in the hole. After the fire died, the wood would be removed from the hole. Food wrapped in bundles was then placed in the hole to be heated by the hot rocks and soil.

Many dishes were prepared like modern stews. The Miwok used watertight baskets instead of pottery bowls. Stones heated in the fire were stirred into the mixture inside the basket. A large wooden paddle was used to keep the hot stones moving.

This photo shows holes in which the Miwok ground acorns and other nuts.

CHAPTER FOUR

WHERE THEY LIVED

Miwok houses were usually built with a circular floor plan. Wooden poles were used as a framework for walls built of reeds, reed mats, and grass. At the center of every home was a fire pit used to cook family meals and heat the house. A hole in the center of the roof allowed smoke to escape and let light in. Some houses were covered with clay to keep them warm and dry during bad weather. The door to each house was covered with a reed mat or animal hide.

Miwok communities had populations of 20 to 200 people. There were two kinds of Miwok communities: hamlets and villages. Hamlets were small settlements where people who were related to each other lived. Villages were larger communities where a headman, or leader, and his family lived.

This Miwok roundhouse shows the circular layout of most Miwok structures. The central fire pit and smoke hole can also be seen here.

The headman's village had a larger structure that served as an assembly hall. These buildings are sometimes called roundhouses. Some measured more than 60 feet (18.3 m) wide and had clay floors that were 5 feet (1.5 m) deep. Four massive upright logs supported the smaller beams that made up the cone-shaped roof.

Most settlements also had a sweat lodge with a large fire in the middle. This fire filled the building with smoke and high heat. Sweat lodges were used for healing and religious ceremonies. The Miwok also built storehouses, or granaries, on wooden platforms or in tree trunks. These were used to preserve food.

Many of the Miwok moved to temporary camps several times each year to take advantage of changing food resources. They built structures there out of grasses, leaves, bark, and reeds.

These temporary Miwok shelters are made from tree bark.

CHAPTER FIVE

SOCIAL STRUCTURE

The smallest Miwok social unit was the family. Each family belonged to one of two larger units called moieties. Each moiety was represented by a common animal ancestor, such as a wildcat or coyote. A reference to a person's moiety was usually included in his or her name. No one was allowed to marry anyone from their own moiety. Two moieties made up the largest Miwok social unit, which is known as a tribelet.

The most powerful Miwok leaders had assistants that helped them communicate and organize community events. Each Miwok headman was helped by a female religious leader sometimes called a dreamer or headwoman. Villages also had people who served as doctors. Doctors gathered sacred objects they believed held special powers. They were respected and feared by other members of the community, who believed they could use their powers to harm people.

Coyotes were featured in many stories told by the Miwok. Coyotes were honored for their cleverness.

CHAPTER SIX

GOVERNMENT

The tribelet was the basic unit of Miwok government. The population of most tribelets ranged from 100 to 500 people. A tribelet's territory included food-gathering and hunting areas, the main village, and related hamlets. The position of headman was passed down from a father to his son.

The headman managed important parts of daily life in the community. He was responsible for paying for major celebrations and hosting visitors. Anyone who wanted to use the tribelet's resources had to ask the headman for permission. He sometimes acted as a judge for family conflicts. Some headmen had a staff of special hunters, fishermen, cooks, and servers. These people helped during religious ceremonies or when outsiders were visiting. The Miwok also had speakers, who were people who took orders directly from the headmen and often ruled over smaller hamlets.

Important meetings were held in roundhouses, such as the building pictured here.

CHAPTER SEVEN

WARFARE

The village headman usually led his warriors in battle. The Miwok protected their land against challenges from other American Indian communities and sometimes launched attacks to gain property and captives. Sometimes wars were started when one community accused another of using magic to cause problems with the **environment**, such as floods. The Miwok used spears and bows and arrows in combat.

Between 1769 and 1880, the Europeans introduced horses to the American Indians. The Miwok tamed horses and learned how to use them as a resource. Riding horses changed the methods used in Miwok warfare. The Europeans also introduced guns, which made warfare deadlier than ever before. With the weapons introduced by the Europeans, conflicts between American Indian communities and clashes with Europeans resulted in greater violence than had existed before.

This Miwok man photographed in 1924 is shown with a spear.

CHAPTER EIGHT

RELIGION

The Miwok religion aimed to help people understand the world and their place in it, focusing on the need to keep the balance between humans and the natural environment. Many hours were spent gathered in roundhouses for community worship. Young people learned about traditions and history from Miwok elders.

They held religious celebrations on many occasions, including acorn harvests, births, and marriages. During the ceremonies, the Miwok generally sang and danced. Religious leaders wore special body paint and colored feather headbands. Music was made using wooden clapper sticks, hollow foot drums, flutes, and whistles.

WOODEN CLAPPER STICK

This photo, which was taken in 1872, shows a group of Miwok people gathered for a religious celebration in the Yosemite Valley.

The modern Miwok preserve hundreds of traditional religious stories. Mount Diablo in western California is still regarded as a sacred place. According to many elders, Grandfather Coyote created the Miwok people, along with everything they needed to survive, at this mountain peak.

CHAPTER NINE

ARTS AND CRAFTS

Some Miwok art may have been inspired by their religious beliefs. The eastern Miwok marked rocky outcroppings with **intricate** designs, such as human tracks, wheels, circles, and similar **geometric** patterns. These images were lightly carved into the rocks. These types of markings are called petroglyphs. They are sacred to many American Indians.

The Miwok made things that were both practical and beautiful. Miwok women were incredible basket makers. They collected special grasses and tree shoots to weave together into different patterns and decorated the baskets using feathers and shells. Bones were transformed into combs, hairpins, beads, and needles. Hemp was used to make thread to weave into bags, belts, and nets. Miwok villagers often traded with their neighbors. They often paid their trading partners in shell beads that served as a kind of money.

This Miwok woman is shown holding a sifting basket. Baskets made by the Miwok were highly prized in trade.

CHAPTER TEN

DEALING WITH THE NEWCOMERS

Juan Rodríguez Cabrillo was the first European to explore the Pacific shoreline of California. In 1542, some of the Coast Miwok saw Cabrillo's ships. He told the American Indians that he was claiming the region for King Carlos I of Spain and that it was now a part of New Spain.

During the 200 years that followed, many other Europeans explored the region. Among them was an Englishman named Sir Francis Drake. He stopped in the Miwok region to repair his ship before continuing his voyage around the world. Drake's expedition provided the first illustrations and descriptions of the Miwok. Although the Europeans didn't start a colony in California until 1769, they brought about many changes before that time. They introduced illnesses such as smallpox, which killed tens of thousands of American Indians.

A monument celebrating Juan Rodríguez Cabrillo now stands in San Diego, California.

CHAPTER ELEVEN

THE SPANISH AND RUSSIAN EMPIRES

In 1776, a military base and **mission** were established in what's now San Francisco. A Spanish naval officer, Joseph Canizares, followed the shoreline into the lands of the Bay Miwok. Most of the foreigners' activities took place in a narrow strip of coastal land that stretched from San Diego to San Francisco. Here they built a chain of military colonies called presidios and towns called pueblos. They also built missions, which were used to spread Christianity and the Spanish way of life. After 1794, large numbers of Coast Miwok, Bay Miwok, and Plains Miwok were drawn into the missions on the shores of San Francisco Bay because their traditional way of life was becoming increasingly difficult to maintain.

In 1812, the Russians established a fort at Bodega Bay. As time passed, the invaders forced many Miwok to work for them as slaves.

Many of California's missions were run by Franciscan monks like the two men pictured here. For some American Indians, the missions offered opportunities for a new way of life. For others, they represented a loss of traditional culture.

CHAPTER TWELVE

A CHANGING WORLD

As Europeans entered California, they brought about changes that made it difficult to continue the traditional Miwok way of life. In 1821, more changes arrived when Mexico claimed control of California. Some Miwok resisted the further invasion of their lands. Violent conflicts led to many deaths. Many lives were also claimed by more disease in 1833.

In 1847, Mexico **ceded** control of California to the United States, making conditions for the Miwok worse than ever. The United States government adopted policies that aimed to remove all American Indian people from California. The discovery of gold in California in 1848 caused an **influx** of settlers that **displaced** the Miwok from their homes. Many were forced to work as slaves. Today, the Miwok lands have been transformed by more than 200 years of the invaders' activities.

Conflict between gold miners and the Miwok resulted in the Mariposa Indian War of 1851. The United States Army defeated the Miwok in this war, forcing them out of the Yosemite Valley. The Miwok were given permission to return to the Yosemite Valley in 1855.

CHAPTER THIRTEEN

THE MIWOK TODAY

Treatment of the Miwok was slow to improve. The United States government set aside a few small areas, called rancherias, for the Coast, Plains, Northern Sierra, and Central Sierra Miwok. In 1924, the United States granted citizenship to all American Indians, partly in recognition for their bravery and sacrifices during World War I. The Miwok renewed their struggle to reclaim their homelands and educate their children.

The Miwok are a proud nation anxious to preserve their **heritage**. Many Miwok people have been at the forefront of the environmental movement throughout their homelands. Some are working hard to correct incorrect **portrayals** of American Indians in television, movies, and classrooms. The Miwok continue to fight for the rights they deserve and to build a better future for their people.

GLOSSARY

cede (SEED) To give control of something to another person or government.

culture (KULL-chur) The beliefs and way of life of a certain group of people.

descendant (dih-SEN-dent) Someone related to a person or group of people who lived at any earlier time.

displace (dis-PLAYS) To force people to leave the area where they live.

environment (en-VY-run-ment) The natural world around us.

geometric (jee-uh-MEH-trik) Having to do with straight lines, circles, and other simple shapes.

heritage (HER-uh-tij) The traditions and beliefs that are part of the history of a group or nation.

influx (IN-flux) An arrival or entry of a large number of people or things.

intricate (IN-trih-kit) Having many parts.

mission (MIH-shun) A community established by a church for the purpose of spreading its faith.

portrayal (por-TRAY-uhl) A picture or representation of someone or something.

primitive (PRIH-muh-tiv) Very simple and basic; not modern and without much skill.

resource (REE-sors) Something that can be used.

INDEX

PRIMARY SOURCE LIST

Page 19
On the Merced–Southern Miwok. Photograph. Taken by Edward S. Curtis in California. ca. 1924. Now kept at the Library of Congress, Prints and Photographs Division, Washington, D.C.

Page 23
Sifting basket–Southern Miwok. Photograph. Taken by Edward S. Curtis in California. ca. 1924. Now kept at the Library of Congress, Prints and Photographs Division, Washington, D.C.

Page 29
Mariposa Indian Encampment, Yosemite Valley, California. Oil on paper. ca. 1872. Created by Albert Bierstadt. ca. 1872. Now kept at the Public Collection, Indianapolis, IN.

WEBSITES

Due to the changing nature of Internet links, PowerKids Press has developed an online list of websites related to the subject of this book. This site is updated regularly. Please use this link to access the list: www.powerkidslinks.com/saic/miw